the journey

Who Is This Jesus?

The Gospel of John (Chapters 1–15)

Charles "Chic" Shaver

BEACON HILL PRESS
OF KANSAS CITY

Copyright 1980, 2009
By Beacon Hill Press of Kansas City

First Edition 1980
Second Edition 2009

ISBN 978-0-8341-2502-5

Cover design: J.R. Caines
Interior design: Sharon Page

10 9 8 7 6 5 4 3 2 1

Contents

1

The Light and the Word
John 1:1–18; 3:16–21; 12:17–36

Prayer

Begin your Bible study with a brief prayer. Ask God to open your hearts and to help you understand His Word.

Opening Thoughts

John 1:14 says, "The Word became flesh and made his dwelling among us." That means God loved His creation enough to send Jesus into the world with all of its ugliness and messiness; God loved us enough to put His Son in that mess, among that sin, right beside us.

The Jews had been waiting for a promised one for years. They needed the word to become truth. The Gentiles were walking in the dark without a hope for the future. They needed a light to guide them. It wouldn't be long after a special baby was born in Bethlehem that people, both Jews and Gentiles, began whispering, wondering, "Who is this Jesus?"

Discuss the Scripture

Read John 1:1-18

1. Find and list 10 or 12 things this scripture says about "The Word."

2. Read verse 1 again replacing "the Word" with "Jesus." What is Jesus' relationship to God? How might Jesus help us understand God better?

3. "The light shines in the darkness, but the darkness has not understood it" (v. 5). What do you think this verse means? Is this still true today?

4. Can you share about a time when someone or something was a "light" to you?

5. Verse 14 says, "The Word became flesh and made his dwelling among us." When did this happen and how does it make our relationship with Christ easier?

Read John 3:16-21

1. John 3:16 is a popular memory verse for children and new believers. Why do you think this verse is so special?

2. Does the world view Jesus as one who came to "condemn the world" or to "save the world"? Why?

3. Read verses 19-21 and replace the word "light" with the word "Jesus." How does this help you better understand who Christ is?

4. Why are humans so apt to love darkness instead of light? Where do you see this portrayed in our society?

5. In what ways can Christians continue to live "by the truth" in "the light" (v. 21)?

Read John 12:17-36

1. How did the principle of life through death apply to Jesus (v. 24)? How does the principle of life through death apply to you?

2. Verse 25 can be confusing. What do you think Jesus is saying here?

3. What does it mean to serve Christ (v. 26)? What are some of the places where serving Christ might take you? What is the end result of following Christ?

4. How was it possible for Jesus to be troubled by "this hour" and committed to it at the same time (v. 27)? How might the same be true for you at some points in your life?

Closing Thoughts

What have you learned in this study that seems the most significant or meaningful to you?

Closing Prayer

As a group, close in prayer, thanking God for what you have learned during this session. Ask Him to continue to speak to you; promise to listen.

2
The Miracle Worker
John 2:1-11; 5:1-15; 11:1-44

Prayer

Begin your Bible study with a brief prayer. Ask God to open your hearts and to help you understand His Word.

Opening Thoughts

Nathanael, one of Christ's early followers, was from Cana, and Jesus takes His disciples there for a wedding. Already He is training His followers. The wedding ceremonies, held at the bridegroom's home, would usually extend over several days. The marriage was important—one of the most significant events in the life of a family. Any failure to entertain the guests properly would cause severe embarrassment.

When the family in this passage runs out of wine, Jesus steps in to help, turning water into wine. No one was hurting and healed. No one was lost and found. No one was lacking understanding and taught. Jesus just helped the family avoid embarrassment. While understanding the plain facts of these events, look for the deeper meaning in Jesus' first miracle. And watch how Mary becomes the first true disciple to believe and act on her belief.

Discuss the Scripture

Read John 2:1-11

Robert Stein clarifies the type of wine mentioned in these verses. He says, "The term 'wine' . . . in the ancient world, then, did not mean wine as we understand it today but wine mixed with water." An example would be three parts water to one part wine. To drink wine unmixed was considered a barbarian custom. "In ancient times there were not many beverages that were safe to drink. . . . The safest and easiest method of making the water safe to drink, however, was to mix it with wine."*

1. Compare the faith of Mary and the faith of the disciples in this passage. When do they believe? Why might their faith be different because of their pasts and how can we apply this to our own lives?

2. The water in the jars (v. 6) was used in the ceremonial washing of hands and feet. Now try to determine the more important spiritual meaning in this miracle. Think of it as a sign of something greater (v. 11).

a. What is the difference between foot-washing water and the best wine?

b. What is the difference between the purification symbolized by water (the old Jewish system) and by wine (the new system brought by Christ)? (See Matt. 26:27-28 and Heb. 1:3.)

---

*Robert H. Stein, "Wine Drinking in New Testament Times," *Christianity Today,* June 20, 1975, 9-11.

c. Was there enough wine after the miracle?

d. Who stands out as the one most responsible for the success of the wedding party?

3. For Jesus to do a miracle, what part do people play (vv. 7-8)? In other words, how does faith fit into the activity of God?

4. What is the obvious and immediate reason Christ did this miracle?

5. What does this say to you about Jesus' concern for the details of your life?

Read John 5:1-15

1. Bethesda was a place where broken, needy people gathered, hoping to be healed. Are there still places like this in our society today? If so, where?

2. What would your relationship to Bethesda have been? Would you have been

Lying, waiting for healing?

A frequent visitor, offering hope to those in need?

A watcher from the sidelines, making sure people were healed properly?

Miles away, wanting to push the thought aside?

Which best describes the way you approach situations like Bethesda?

3. Who or what was the man in verse 7 depending on? Do you ever feel like this man during difficult situations?

4. What three commands does Jesus give the lame man in verse 8? What is the man's response? How do you think you would have responded? What should you do if Jesus tells you to do something that seems impossible?

5. What is Jesus' expectation—both then and today—of one who has been healed either physically or spiritually (v. 14)?

Read John 11:1-44

1. Mary and Martha have mixed feelings toward Jesus because He did not come when or do what they expected (vv. 17-44). How can we identify with them and learn from their relationships with Christ?

2. This is a passage when it is obvious that Christ is both fully human and fully God. What does that mean and how is it shown in this passage?

3. "The glory of God" (v. 40) may be understood as God's power shining through our experiences. Do you recall some time when you saw the glory of God revealed in the circumstances of your life?

4. What does Jesus mean by His prayer in John 11:41-42? How was Jesus able to pray with such certainty? (See 1 John 5:14-15.)

5. What happens when Jesus' power meets death's power? How does this make you feel when you know that Jesus is present today?

Closing Thoughts

What have you learned in this study that seems the most significant or meaningful to you?

Closing Prayer

As a group, close in prayer, thanking God for what you have learned during this session. Ask Him to continue to speak to you; promise to listen.

3

Living Water and the Bread of Life

John 4:4–39; 6:1–15; 6:26–69

Prayer

Begin your Bible study with a brief prayer. Ask God to open your hearts and to help you understand His Word.

Opening Thoughts

The two stories in this chapter are vastly different. In one, Jesus speaks with a woman whose need is as deep as the well they meet at. She is lonely, empty, longing, *thirsty*. The need here is spiritual and personal. In the next story, Jesus feeds thousands of people who are hungry because they have hung around to hear Jesus speak and missed dinner. Their stomachs are growling, they are complaining, they are *hungry*. The need here is physical and vast.

These two stories show how deep and wide Christ's love truly is. When Jesus refers to himself as water or bread, He is demonstrating that He knows we are thirsty, hungry beings. The reality of the Word becoming flesh is that God can be experienced through the senses. We taste and touch material things. He knows we are born empty and needy, and He tells us our hunger and thirst can be met in Him. Just like the woman at the well and the crowd without food, Jesus can fill us; He alone can meet our needs.

Discuss the Scripture

Read John 4:4-39

1. When the woman requests water in verse 15, why does Jesus reply to her as He does in verse 16?

2. In verse 28, the Samaritan woman leaves her water pot. In view of John's symbolic use of water, what is the possible meaning of that act? What would be comparable to the water pot in your life—something you left when you met Christ?

3. Knowing what Jesus tells us about this woman's life, it's safe to assume she might have a reputation in her town. Why is it significant that Jesus uses her to announce His presence and spread His message?

4. What is another way of saying, "My food . . . is to do the will of him who sent me" (v. 34)? Can you recall a time you did the will of God and the satisfaction you experienced? If you are willing to, share that experience with the group.

5. How might your life be different if you truly followed Jesus' command to "open your eyes and look at the fields" (v. 35)?

Read John 6:1-15

1. What was Jesus' purpose in going to the hillside or mountain? How did the unexpected arrival of the crowd affect His plan?

2. How do the interruptions in our lives become God's teaching tools?

3. How do Philip and Andrew respond to the problem of the hungry crowd differently (vv. 7-9)? When you face a problem that seems insurmountable, is your approach more like Philip's or Andrew's?

4. What is the extent of human need, both then and now? What is the extent of God's power to fulfill that need, both then and now?

5. Why would Jesus worry about the leftovers (vv. 12-13)?

Read John 6:26-69

1. As you examine your own attitudes, what would you say are your motives for following Christ (vv. 61-69)? In other words, is Christ a means to an end, or is He the end?

2. What indications are there that human effort alone is not enough for a person to come to Christ (vv. 37, 44, 65)?

3. How would your life change if you took Christ into your spirit as you take food into your body?

4. Why are people offended both then and now at teachings like vv. 53-58?

5. Jesus ultimately understood that humans are hungry beings. What are we hungry for and how can Jesus alone fill those needs?

Closing Thoughts

What have you learned in this study that seems the most significant or meaningful to you?

Closing Prayer

As a group, close in prayer, thanking God for what you have learned during this session. Ask Him to continue to speak to you; promise to listen.

4

A Man of Controversy
John 5:16-30; 7:37-52; 9:13-41

Prayer

Begin your Bible study with a brief prayer. Ask God to open your hearts and to help you understand His Word.

Opening Thoughts

Many Christians have heard about Jesus referred to as the Son, the Good Shepherd, or the Bread of Life, but not many realize how much controversy surrounded Him during His time on earth. There must have been an electric atmosphere in Jerusalem when Jesus showed up. The Jews were watching for Him, and the crowds were whispering about Him. The amazing claims He made were hard for many people to understand. And yet they had been waiting and praying for the Promised One for many, many years. What was it that made it so hard for so many to accept Jesus when He finally came? The passages in this chapter deal directly with the opposition Jesus faced during His days on earth.

Discuss the Scripture

Read John 5:16-30

1. The Bible tells us that God rested on the Sabbath from His labors of creating the physical world. Why then does Jesus say He is always working (v. 17)?

2. If you had lived during Jesus' days and had encountered Him, do you think your reaction would have been more like the Jews in this passage or the Samaritan woman (see 4:28-29)?

3. There are many references to the Son and the Father in this passage. How does this passage help you gain new insight into the relationship of Jesus and God? What responsibility has the Father handed over completely to the Son and why (5:22, 27)?

4. In verse 29, doing good is named as the condition for rising to life. But in verse 24 Jesus stressed belief as the condition for eternal life. How are "doing good" and "faith" related? (See Eph. 2:8-10.)

5. What do you think Jesus said that was most troubling to the Jews who were listening to Him and why? Read John 5:39-40 and discuss why Jesus was also frustrated by this encounter.

Read John 7:37-52

1. Verse 43 says, "Thus the people were divided because of Jesus." What caused them to be divided?

2. What part do humans today have in making Jesus either a unifying force or dividing force in the world we live in? (See Matt. 10:34.)

3. What do you think the real reasons were that the people rejected Jesus? What excuses do people today offer for not accepting Jesus?

4. Why don't the guards bring Jesus in (vv. 45-46)? Why is this so frustrating to the Pharisees?

5. Why were the Pharisees so threatened by Jesus?

Read John 9:13-41

1. Look at verse 25. What does the man say in his testimony that gives you clues about how to witness about the good news of Christ?

2. What does Jesus do when others treat us unfairly because of our faith (v. 35)?

3. What is the double meaning in the words, "You have now seen him" (v. 37)?

4. Verses 39-41 can be confusing. Who are the real blind people in this text? What is it that they do not see? How do you "get sight" about your own blindness?

5. In what way does seeing Jesus in the midst of controversy in these passages impact your relationship with Him?

Closing Thoughts

What have you learned in this study that seems the most significant or meaningful to you?

Closing Prayer

As a group, close in prayer, thanking God for what you have learned during this session. Ask Him to continue to speak to you; promise to listen.

5

The Good Shepherd and the Vine

John 10:1-13; 10:25-30; 15:1-17

Prayer

Begin your Bible study with a brief prayer. Ask God to open your hearts and to help you understand His Word.

Opening Thoughts

The pastureland of Judea was a central plateau, about 35 miles long and 15 miles wide. The plateau drops off sharply on each side. Because of the dangers, sheep would never be turned out to graze without a shepherd who was always on duty to protect them from both thieves and wild animals. The shepherd carried a sling. He was so accurate with this that he could fire a stone in front of the nose of a straying sheep and turn it back. A short club and a shepherd's crook were also part of his equipment.

Because the sheep were raised mainly for wool, a shepherd and his sheep would work together for years. He often named them according to their physical characteristics. In the fields, he would walk ahead of the sheep to encourage them to follow him. The shepherd often used a sing-song call to summon his flock. They came to know his voice so well that they would not respond to a stranger's voice.

Discuss the Scripture

Read John 10:1-13

1. What is the spiritual meaning for you in the phrase, "He calls his own sheep by name" (v. 3)?

2. What is the spiritual meaning for you in the phrase, "He goes on ahead of them, and his sheep follow him because they know his voice" (v. 4)?

3. How do you know Jesus' voice when you hear it? Can you share a time when you heard His voice and responded?

4. What is the difference in the thief's interest in the sheep and the shepherd's interest (especially vv. 10-11)?

5. Throughout the passage, Christ names some things that make Him the Good Shepherd. Name these and tell how you've seen them demonstrated in your own life.

Read John 10:25-30

1. Mark 6:34 says, "He had compassion on them [a large crowd], because they were like sheep without a shepherd." What is life like for sheep without a shepherd? Compare this to a life without Christ.

2. Now think about what life is like for sheep who have a shepherd. Compare this to a life with Christ.

3. What three things does Jesus promise to His sheep (v. 28)?

4. In John 10:27, "listen" and "follow" are present tense verbs. This means that following the Good Shepherd is a continual process. What must you do to continue to follow Him?

5. There are many things and people in this life that may attempt to lead you astray. Name some of these things/people. What should your response be to something or someone who is trying to take you away from Jesus?

Read John 15:1-17

1. Why does the Father trim or prune fruit-bearing branches (v. 2)? Think of a time when you went through a pruning experience. How did you feel and what were the results?

2. Fruit is mentioned in other places in the Bible. Read John 15:16; Col. 1:6; and Gal. 5:22-23. Talk about what it means to bear fruit.

3. In practical daily living, how do you remain in Christ?

4. What brings a Christian joy according to John 15:9-11? Can you remember a time in your life when you felt extreme joy or felt like you had no joy? How did that correspond with your walk with Christ?

5. In verse 15, what is the difference between servants and friends? What category do you feel you are in? Why?

Closing Thoughts

What have you learned in this study that seems the most significant or meaningful to you?

Closing Prayer

As a group, close in prayer, thanking God for what you have learned during this session. Ask Him to continue to speak to you; promise to listen.

6

The Way, the Truth, and the Life
John 13:31—14:14

Prayer

Begin your Bible study with a brief prayer. Ask God to open your hearts and to help you understand His Word.

Opening Thoughts

Many writers throughout the ages have used what are called universal images to connect readers across cultures and across time. Many of the names Jesus uses to refer to himself in John are universal images—things that any person, anywhere, any time can understand and relate to. Bread and water, light and darkness, son and father, shepherd and sheep. Talk about these universal images as you study the names that tell us who Jesus is, and think about how you were on His mind when He used these images way back then.

Also, keep in mind that the idea of "the way" connects to the Old Testament law, which served as the way the people of God were to live in obedience. Jesus becomes not only the fulfillment of the law but also the new and living way of the people of God.

Discuss the Scripture

Read John 13:31—14:14

1. As Jesus begins to speak in John 13:31, He knows that He will soon be leaving earth. How does this increase the importance of His message? Does there seem to be a new level of desperation in this passage?

2. The world we live in can almost promise that we will have troubled hearts at one point or another. But in John 14:1 Jesus says, "Do not let your hearts be troubled." What assurance does Jesus give following that command to help us avoid troubled hearts?

3. What is the value of doubts and questions like Thomas had in verse 5?

4. Compare John 10:9 with John 14:6. How are these life-changing verses?

5. In what way is John 14:12 a call to action? How faithful have you been to this call to action?

6. What promise does Jesus make to His disciples in John 14:14? How does this promise make you feel?

Review

1. Below is a list of names for Christ that have been covered in this study. Spend some time as a group discussing each name and what you learned about the characteristics of Jesus from the names used for Him.

The Light

The Word

The Miracle Worker

The Son of God

The Son of Man

The Living Water

The Bread of Life

The Good Shepherd

The Gate

The Vine

The Way

The Truth

The Life

2. Which one of these names for Christ seems the most meaningful to you? Why?

3. Are there other names you've heard used for Jesus? What are they and what do they mean to you?

4. Think back on the people you've encountered in the stories of John: the family of the wedding in Cana, the Samaritan woman at the well, the lame man at the pool of Bethesda, the five thousand fed, the blind man who was healed, Lazarus, Mary and Martha, the disciples, the religious leaders. Which characters do you identify with most and why?

5. After studying the Book of John, how would you answer the question, "Who is Jesus?"

Closing Thoughts
What have you learned in this study that seems the most significant or meaningful to you?

Closing Prayer
As a group, close in prayer, thanking God for what you have learned during this session. Ask Him to continue to speak to you; promise to listen.

www.ingramcontent.com/pod-product-compliance
Lightning Source LLC
Chambersburg PA
CBHW060548030426
42337CB00021B/4491